# CARNIVOROUS PLANTS

# CARNIVOROUS
# PLANTS

## BY NANCY J. NIELSEN

A First Book
Franklin Watts
New York/London/Toronto/Sydney

Cover photograph copyright © Breck P. Kent

Photographs copyright ©: Breck P. Kent: pp. 2, 17, 24; Joe Mazrimas:
p. 8; Comstock Photography, Inc.: pp. 11, 40 (both Michael
S. Thompson), 31 (Sharon Chester), 33, 41, 45, 47, 50, 53
(all Gwen Fidler), 35, 48 (both Townsend P. Dickinson);
Animals Animals/Earth Scenes: pp. 13, 28 (both Zig Leszczynski),
21 (Peter Parks/OSF), 26 (G. I. Bernard/OSF); U.S. Fish and Wildlife
Service, Washington, D.C.: pp. 16 (J.D. Pittillo), 51 (Porter B. Reed, Jr.);
Kohout Productions/Root Resources: 28 inset, 38; Ben Fischman: p. 55.

Library of Congress Cataloging-in-Publication Data

Nielsen, Nancy J.
Carnivorous plants / by Nancy J. Nielsen.
p.   cm. — (A First book)
Includes bibliographical references and index.
Summary: Describes various plants that prey on animals, including
the Venus Fly Trap, bladderwort, and pitcher plant.
ISBN 0-531-20056-6
1. Carnivorous plants—Juvenile literature.   [1. Carnivorous
plants.]   I. Title.   II. Series.
QK917.N54   1992
581.5'3—dc20                                         91-34422 CIP AC

# CONTENTS

# CARNIVOROUS PLANTS

*Magnified view of the waterwheel plant (Aldrovanda).
A tiny insect trap forms the end of each leaf.*

# INTRODUCTION: WHAT ARE CARNIVOROUS PLANTS?

The little white flowers of a waterwheel plant (*Aldrovanda*) float on the surface of a small pond. Under the water, tiny clam-shaped leaves are attached in groups of eight to a stem. The leaves of the 6-inch (15-cm) rootless plant are shaped somewhat like the waterwheel it is named after.

No one would guess that such a harmless-looking plant could be so deadly to small animals. The leaves, less than ¼ inch (0.6 cm) long, each bear a miniature trap smaller than the tip of a sharpened pencil. A small insect larva bumps up against small trigger hairs. Suddenly the two sides of the leaf (called *lobes*) snap shut, and the larva is trapped inside. Then the waterwheel plant slowly digests

9

the small animal. In a few days it will reopen to catch other larvae, or water fleas or small plankton.

Plants that prey on animals are called *carnivorous* (meat-eating) plants. There are fifteen *genera* (groups) of carnivorous plants on earth. Most genera can be divided into many variations called *species*. If all are counted separately, over 500 species of carnivorous plants can be found. The Croatan National Forest in North Carolina has the widest selection of carnivorous plants of any area in the United States.

Carnivorous plants vary from tiny plants to species that grow to 3 feet (90 cm) tall or more. Most grow on boggy land, not in water. The leaves often grow close to the ground and are sometimes arranged in a *rosette* (rose-shaped) or pinwheel fashion. A tall stalk will grow from the center of the rosette in spring or early summer. The stalk bears beautiful flowers.

The leaves of carnivorous plants serve as the traps that lure and capture animals. Some plants,

*Many carnivorous plants, such as these sundew plants from Australia, have leaves that are arranged in a rosette (rose-shaped) pattern.*

like the waterwheel, have active, fast-moving traps. Others have "flypaper" traps and catch their prey with a sticky, glue-like substance. Still other carnivorous plants are passive and do not move at all. Instead, a sweet nectar attracts small animals inside the plants' pitcher-shaped leaves. Once they have crawled in, the animals find that they cannot get out again.

When the prey is captured, the leaves serve as stomachs that digest it. If we think of eating in the sense of using a mouth or teeth for chewing, then we cannot say that carnivorous plants actually *eat* animals. They do not have mouths or teeth. Instead, parts or all of the trapped animals are broken down into a liquid by the leaves' special bacteria or digestive juices. This mixture of protein, minerals, and digestive juices is sometimes called a broth or a soup. It is absorbed through the leaves for its nutritive content.

*Botanists* (scientists who study plants) speculate that carnivorous plants became meat-eating in or-

*Boggy habitats are nitrogen-poor. As a result, such plants as the bladderworts pictured here developed means of obtaining nitrogen from the bodies of insects.*

der to adapt to their environment. Green plants make their own food using sunlight and water. They also require nutrients, which they get from the water and soil. But most carnivorous plants live in bogs where the soil is poor in nutrients, especially *nitrogen*. If the plants do not have a source for nitrogen, they cannot produce their own food and will die.

How did carnivorous plants develop this ability? Adrian Slack, a writer and plant expert, suggests that one day a plant growing in boggy, nitrogen-poor soil collected a bit of rainwater in a bowl-shaped leaf. An insect then landed in the rainwater and drowned, and its body decomposed. The nitrogen from the insect's body was absorbed into the plant through the leaves. As long as the plant was able to get nitrogen in this fashion it could continue to live in nitrogen-poor soil.

Modern expansion poses a threat to carnivorous plants. As urban areas continue to expand, many swamps and bogs are being drained and turned into housing developments. Many carnivorous plants are being preserved in greenhouses where they are easy to grow. Still, it is important that swamps and bogs be preserved so we do not lose any of these species of unusual and interesting plants.

# CHAPTER 2

# VENUS'S-FLYTRAPS

The snap-trap leaves of the Venus's-flytrap (*Dionaea muscipula*) lie deceptively still on a clump of dirt in the middle of a swamp. An ant is attracted to their brilliant red color and sweet-tasting nectar. As the ant crawls inside one of the clam-shaped leaves, its body scrapes against the leaf's trigger hairs. Suddenly, the leaf snaps shut, trapping the ant inside.

The leaves of a Venus's-flytrap can snap shut in less than one second. They are the best-known of the carnivorous plants.

As the ant struggles to free itself, it actually aids in its own digestion. The more the insect wiggles about, the more tightly closed the trap becomes and the faster its glands release their digestive juices.

*Above: A cluster of Venus's-flytraps await its prey.*
*Facing: This sequence of photos shows the stages in an*
*insect's demise at the hands of a Venus's-flytrap.*

1          2

3          4

only 2, 3, and 4

The trap will remain closed for 8–10 days. When it reopens, all that is left of the ant is a skeleton, which the wind soon blows away. Then the trap is ready for its next victim.

Even though Venus's-flytraps are known and studied throughout the world, they grow in only one area—the swamps of North and South Carolina. The 3-inch-long (7.6 cm) leaves form a rosette that fans out in all directions, making the plant about 6 inches (15 cm) across. Each leaf consists of two winglike lobes joined with a hinge and edged with long, stiff bristles—the perfect trap! The stem and outer leaves are green, but the inner part of the traps are bright red.

In the winter Venus's-flytraps lie dormant, but in spring a stem grows to about 1 foot (30 cm) tall and bears white flowers. The tall stem contains none of the deadly traps. The flowers' seeds will be dispersed eventually by the wind. Those that land undisturbed in moist bog soil will grow into new Venus's-flytraps.

One of the most unusual characteristics about Venus's-flytraps is their trigger hairs. On the inside of each lobe grow three to four short hairs. If something touches just one of these trigger hairs, nothing will happen. This is assumed to protect the trap from snapping shut when touched by a blade of

## How to Grow Venus's-flytraps

Venus's-flytraps are popular house- and greenhouse plants because they are easy to grow. They can be grown from seeds or bulbs, or can be purchased already potted.

Because Venus's-flytraps are bog plants, they need lots of water. The pot in which they are planted should be set in a pan filled with 1½ inches (3.8 cm) of water. Rainwater or distilled water must be used, as chemicals from faucet water (such as fluoride or chlorine) will kill them. Venus's-flytraps can even be submerged in water and still thrive!

Venus's-flytraps need lots of sunlight, especially during spring and summer. They should be placed in a south window if possible. In winter the plants need less light as they become *dormant* (inactive).

The soil for flytraps must be as close as possible to the kind of soil that would be found in a bog. It can be made by mixing two parts peat moss with one part sand. Most flytraps should be repotted soon after purchasing, as the plants need plenty of root space. Also, repotting them can ensure that they have the kind of soil they need. Venus's-flytraps should only be repotted in the spring or summer when the plant is in full growth.

Because Venus's-flytraps get their nutrients from digesting insects, they require very little fertilizer or plant food. Instead, they feed on unwanted house ants, spiders, or flies.

grass or a drop of rain. When two or more hairs are touched within seconds of each other, however, the trap will snap shut. If a trap is fooled into closing on something it can't eat such as a small twig or stone, it will gradually reopen within 24 hours.

How does the leaf close? Scientists have studied this to find out. Evidently, touching the trigger hairs sends an electric impulse throughout the leaf, setting off a chain reaction. First the leaf's cells become stimulated. Then they expand like balloons. Their sudden, explosive growth causes the trap to snap shut.

In order for the trap to work effectively, it must be able to close completely. This is to seal the prey

shrink →

Venus's-flytraps
do not only trap
insects. Here a
young frog falls
prey to one of
these plants.

off from outside air and completely surround it with the digestive juices, which also prevent decay.

A leaf that traps an insect longer than ¼ inch (0.6 cm) will have trouble closing. Then the dead insect will begin to rot, and the rotting will spread to the trap and kill it as well.

Although named *flytraps*, their main food is ants. Venus's-flytraps also eat flies and any other insects they manage to capture, including bees and moths. They have also been known to consume small shrimp when the area in which they grow is flooded with ocean water.

Each trap on a plant can catch and digest three meals before it withers and dies. Then the plant will grow a new trap. The plant experiences a growth spurt each time it captures and digests an insect.

# CHAPTER 3

# BLADDERWORTS

A water flea is swimming about in a pond, looking for something to eat. It is attracted to the antennae of a tiny bladderwort (*Utricularia*), thinking they and the surrounding hairs are algae. Soon the flea becomes sucked into the plant's hollow trap.

The bladderwort's hairs grow from tiny balloon-shaped traps called bladders. The bladders, attached to underwater stems like the traps on a waterwheel, are so tiny that they can barely be seen without a microscope. Still they serve as excellent traps. Like the leaves of a Venus's-flytrap, they are equipped with trigger hairs. A bladder's short, stiff trigger hairs are found at the opening of a trapdoor that opens only one way—inside.

To unsuspecting prey, the bladderwort plant resembles algae. Its traps are the visible balloon-like bladders.

While waiting for its prey, the transparent bladder trap lies flat and empty of water. When the water flea brushes up against the trigger hairs, however, the trapdoor falls open. As water rushes in, so does the water flea. The bladder swells up like a water-filled balloon. Then the trapdoor closes, trapping its victim inside. Like the trap of a Venus's-flytrap, all of this happens in a fraction of a second. *This happens fast,*

The bladderwort lets most of the water out through its walls. Then it digests the water flea, using its digestive juices. This may take it only 15–30 minutes, or as long as a day or two. The juices generally dissolve the entire animal. Sometimes, however, a skeleton is left inside the bladder. Afterward, the bladder flattens itself out again and waits for its next prey.

Besides eating water fleas, bladderworts also capture and digest mosquito larvae and tiny one-celled water organisms. Sometimes they even catch small tadpoles. If the tadpole doesn't fit completely inside a bladder, the plant will first digest the part that fits, later sucking the rest of the tadpole inside to be digested also. Digesting such large prey is hard on the bladder, though, and may cause it to die.

Each bladder traps and digests about fifteen times before it dies. Older bladders may be found to

*← this shrink*

be filled up with the skeletons of the animals it has eaten. New bladders quickly grow to take the place of the old ones, so each plant always contains many bladders.

Bladderworts grow everywhere in the world. There are over 200 species of bladderworts, 20 of which grow in the United States. The species vary in flower color from blue to yellow, purple, or white. Most of them live in water, but a few grow on the ground, especially in bogs.

Bladderworts have no roots, only stems and branches that are so thin they resemble green thread. Certain species grow to 8 inches (20 cm) long. Those that grow in water usually float, but a few become attached to dirt or rocks. Their bladders differ in size, but the largest are only ¼ inch (0.6 cm) wide!

A special kind of bladderwort in South America grows among the dead debris at the bottom of the forest. There the bladders are covered with damp earth and trap small insects that live in the dirt. Other kinds of South American bladderworts live on moss or trees. All of them capture small animals as food.

*A cluster of bladders*

Bladderworts can be found most easily in the United States when their flowers are blooming in midsummer. Look for purple or yellow flowers growing from small streams, ponds, or water-filled ditches. A careful examination of the underwater stems will reveal if they are bladderworts or not. One species of bladderwort that grows in the northern regions has stems containing both bladders and smooth, flat green leaves.

If you have a pond, lake, or swamp nearby, you may have bladderworts growing in your neighborhood. To grow them, you can order bladderworts through certain garden catalogs in the spring or summer.

*The lovely flowers of the bladderwort can be seen in midsummer. They are a handy aid in spotting and identifying these plants.*

# CHAPTER 4

## SUNDEWS

(4)

The leaves of a sundew (*Drosera*) are covered with tentacles tipped with a sticky, sweet nectar. A large fly is attracted to the sweet-smelling nectar. As it approaches the leaf, its wings get stuck in the sticky juice. The more the fly struggles, the more it becomes stuck to the sundew's leaf.

The sundew is a flypaper trap and does not move as quickly as a waterwheel, Venus's-flytrap, or bladderwort. But its tentacles slowly bend toward the fly. In some kinds of sundews, the leaves will actually curl around their victim.

When the fly is completely trapped by the sticky juice, the tentacles secrete digestive juices that digest the fly. The leaves will open again in 4–5 days.

Sundews act as flypaper traps
to capture their prey.

Although carnivorous, a sundew is a plant known for its beauty. The nectar-tipped tentacles sparkle like jewels in the sun. In the morning, their sticky juices can easily be mistaken for dewdrops. The leaves of a sundew are green, but the tentacles and juices have a pretty reddish tinge.

Over ninety species of sundews thrive worldwide. They can be found in Asia, Australia, South Africa, North America, and Europe. The largest grow in Australia, up to 3 feet (90 cm) tall. Aside from trapping all kinds of insects, they often trap small animals such as mice.

Charles Darwin, the great English scientist of the nineteenth century, experimented with sundews. He found that they would eat small amounts of hamburger. His son, Francis Darwin, also experimented with sundews to prove that they are carnivorous. Francis fed insects to one group of sundews but kept another group free of insects. The sundews that were fed insects grew taller and were healthier than the others.

Four common U.S. species of sundews are known as the *roundleaf, spoonleaf, narrowleaf,* and *threadleaf.* Roundleaf and spoonleaf sundews are named for their shapes. They are both called "passive" sundews because, although their tentacles move toward their prey, the leaf itself does not curl or close.

shrink

*Sundew with captured insect. The sticky
juices that cover its leaves can
easily be mistaken for dewdrops.*

Both the narrowleaf and threadleaf sundews are called "active" sundews. They have long, narrow leaves that curl up and over their prey, trapping them inside. The leaves of the threadleaf sundews are even narrower than those of the narrowleaf sundews. They have long thread-like leaves that grow in many directions. These leaves may actually coil around an insect twice to expose more of the insect's body to the plant's digestive juices.

Each leaf can capture and digest three or more victims before dying. Then a new leaf sprouts to take its place. Even small sundews can capture a wide variety of insects, from ants to flies, moths, and butterflies. Like the Venus's-flytrap, they are not fooled by nonfood items such as rocks and twigs.

Some species can catch and digest many insects at one time. Once, about 100 insects were counted stuck to a tall 15-inch-high (38 cm) variety.

The four U.S. species mentioned above are all no more than 6–8 inches (15–20 cm) tall. They are often hard to find, because they are hidden by

*A narrowleaf sundew in West Quoddy Head State Park in Maine*

larger plants. Like the Venus's-flytrap, their leaves hug the ground. Tall stalks grow in the spring and summer and bear beautiful pink or white flowers.

Sundews are hardy plants, often the first to grow back after a forest fire. Those that grow in a cold climate are able to survive the winter by becoming reduced to a small bud.

If you find sundews growing in the United States, don't pick them. In most states they are protected by law.

### How to Grow Sundews

If you wish to cultivate sundews, you must buy them or their seeds. The Cape sundew is easy to grow.

Sundews can also be grown from leaf or root cuttings. If you know someone who cultivates sundews, ask if you can take a couple of leaves home with you. Then cut the leaves into small pieces and place them cut-side down in a soil appropriate for a bog plant. The soil must be covered with sphagnum moss. Water the plants liberally. Within a month or so, a new sundew will grow.

# CHAPTER 5

# BUTTERWORTS

A butterwort (*Pinguicula*) is a small, simple plant. It is the most innocent-looking of all plants that eat insects. Its tentacles are so tiny that it can eat only small insects such as gnats and fruit flies, and small spiders.

A gnat is attracted to the yellow-green plant because of its musty smell. The smell comes from the sticky juices that ooze from tiny glands on each leaf. These juices give the leaf a glistening, almost butter-like appearance.

When the gnat crawls or lands on a butterwort leaf, its legs get stuck in the sticky glue. The more it struggles, the more glue the plant produces. Then the plant's leaves curl toward its victim. The

Butterwort leaves trap insects with a sticky, gluelike substance, which eventually suffocates the insect. Then the leaves, which have been slowly curving inward, release digestive juices.

leaves do not move fast, and they do not trap the gnat. Instead, they simply bring more sticky glue in contact with the gnat's body. Soon the gnat is completely covered with the sticky substance and suffocates.

Then the leaf releases its digestive juices. These juices dissolve the gnat's body into a broth. The broth, which contains nitrogen and other nutrients, is absorbed by the leaf.

The leaf stays curled for a couple of days. When it uncurls, the wind blows away any of the victim's remains.

Like Venus's-flytraps and sundews, butterworts have a neat, round rosette shape. They grow close to the ground and send out tall stems from which white, yellow, mauve, or purple flowers grow in the spring or early summer. Some species are reduced to a small tight bud in winter. Because they grow in bogs and have purple flowers, they are sometimes called bog violets.

Butterworts are found almost everywhere in the northern half of the earth. There are over fifty species, but the species are all very similar. They thrive on moss, wet logs, or damp sand.

Most butterworts grow to about 2 inches (5 cm) in diameter. Some of the larger varieties, however, will grow to 8 inches (20 cm) in diameter. Leaves are usually about ½ inch (1.3 cm) long.

*Left: A purple-flowered butterwort*
*Above: A sundew growing side by side with a butterwort*

Like other carnivorous plants, butterworts seem to know whether or not something that lands on them contains nitrogen. The leaves do not curl up when touched by raindrops, for example. But unlike other carnivorous plants, they will curl up and digest small seeds and other leaves, anything that contains nitrogen. The curling up prevents the leaf from losing its dinner to a strong wind or the rain from washing it away.

Large insects are not endangered by the innocent-looking butterwort. It can only eat small insects.

Butterworts are one of the few carnivorous plants that are helpful to humans. For many years, people dropped butterwort leaves into milk to curdle it. Then the curdled milk was made into butter or cheese. In some rural areas of the world, butterwort is still used to curdle milk. Laplanders (nomadic people who live in Finland) make a gelatin-like dessert by combining butterwort leaves with reindeer milk.

Butterwort leaves also have healing qualities. Farmers have put the leaves on the open wounds of cattle or other farm animals. Modern scientists think the leaves get their medicinal qualities from an antibiotic-like substance in the digestive juices of the leaf. This substance is what keeps an insect from decaying while it is being digested.

Although butterworts prey on small animals, they are also the victims of many larger animals. Slugs, snails, wood lice, leatherjackets (a kind of fish), and aphids all eat and destroy butterworts.

## How to Grow Butterworts

Butterworts are easily grown at home, and can be sprouted from leaves in the same manner as sundews. Simply tear off a leaf, being careful to include its white stem, and place it on sphagnum moss with the cut portion buried. Make sure the moss is kept moist and the cutting is in a bright area but shaded from direct sunlight. It may take several weeks before you notice any growth.

# CHAPTER 6

# PITCHER PLANTS

A grasshopper lands on the rim of an unusual-looking leaf, shaped like a pitcher of water. The sweet nectar secreted by glands near the pitcher's rim draws the grasshopper further inside the leaf. But the wall of the pitcher is also slippery, and the grasshopper slides down into the pitcher.

The grasshopper realizes what has happened, and tries to escape. But downward-pointing stiff hairs make travel out of the pitcher impossible. The only choice the grasshopper has is to travel further down the neck of the pitcher. Soon it loses its footing on the slippery surface and falls into a pool of liquid below. This liquid is often called trap water or "soup." It contains bacteria and/or digestive

A green lynx spider
falls victim to a pitcher
plant in Big Thicket
National Preserve, Texas.

juices. The grasshopper drowns in the soup. Minerals from its body are absorbed into the plant. The grasshopper's skeleton joins many other skeletons collected at the bottom of the pitcher.

Pitcher plants sit passively in open fields in boggy areas. They have no snap traps, and their leaves do not curl. Yet many insects and even larger animals are captured by these colorful but deadly plants with the sweet nectar at their rims.

There are five genera and over eighty species of pitcher plants, which grow mostly in North America and Asia. All have pitcher-shaped leaves and underground stems called *rhizomes* (RYE-zomes). The leaves, like the leaves of other carnivorous plants, form a rosette shape. Large, colorful flowers grow from tall stems in the spring or summer. Unlike the flowers of other carnivorous plants, the flowers of most pitcher plants hang facedown from the stem, like sunflowers do.

All pitcher plants have "hoods" or flaps that hang above the opening of the pitchers. Botanists believe that the purpose of the hoods or flaps is to keep out rainwater that might otherwise fill the pitchers.

Common in the United States is the northern, or purple, pitcher plant (*Sarracenia purpurea*). It can be found along the Atlantic coastline or near fresh

*Trumpet pitcher plants in a field are
"passive" traps to unsuspecting insects.
They do not have to "snap" shut, nor do
their leaves curl around their prey.*

*Another species of pitcher plant* (Sarracenia purpurea) *in a sphagnum bog*

water in the midwestern states. The northern pitcher has curved pitchers that are green with red veins. The plant is an evergreen, meaning that it does not lose its leaves or green color in winter. Its red velvety flowers are shaped somewhat like sunflowers and grow on stems high above the ground. Native Americans used northern pitcher plants as medicinal folk remedies.

The smallest pitcher plants measure only 2–3 inches (5–8 cm) high. The tallest variety of pitcher plant is the huntsman's-horn, which is trumpet-shaped. Its tall, thin leaves can reach a height of 3 feet (90 cm). Larger animals such as frogs and snakes have been captured and digested in these large traps.

The pitcher plants found in Asia and Australia are called *Nepenthes*. They grow only in tropical regions. One, the King Monkey Cup (*N. rajah*), has such large pitchers that it can capture and digest animals as large as rats. Other tropical pitcher plants climb like vines to the tops of trees, or lie flat on the ground.

The cobra lily (*Darlingtonia california*) is a type of pitcher plant that is found only in Oregon and northern California. It has a hood and a small "mouth" out of which hangs a part called a *fishtail* that looks like a cobra's fangs. In addition, the plant

*Left: The flowers of most
pitcher plants hang facedown.
Above: A field of cobra lilies (Darlingtonia),
a type of pitcher plant found in
northern California and Oregon*

has a spiral, bent shape that moves in the wind just like a cobra. Insects are attracted to the cobra lily's fishtail by its sweet nectar. Once inside, they fly around until they are exhausted, unable to find their way out again. The soup at the bottom of a cobra lily contains no digestive juices like some of the other pitcher plants have. Instead, the bodies of the victims are broken down by bacteria. Then the minerals, including nitrogen, are absorbed into the plant.

The parrot pitcher (*Sarracenia psittacina*) is similar to the cobra lily but does not have a fishtail. Instead, it has a small, beak-like opening through which insects crawl. The parrot pitcher is spotted with transparent areas called "windows" that let in more light. When the insects try to leave, they mistake the "windows" for openings, and cannot find their way out of the trap. Soon they fall exhausted into the liquid soup in the bottom of the leaf.

Even though pitcher plants are deadly to many insects and animals, there are a number of animals that make themselves at home in the pitcher plant. Among these are exyra moths, which seem to suffer no ill effects from the pitcher's deadly trap water. Instead they are hatched as larvae from eggs inside the pitchers. They spend their entire lives inside the plant, going through the cocoon and cat-

*A fly atop a pitcher plant*

erpillar stages there. Even as adults, they do not leave the pitcher. Instead they feast on the pitcher plant itself, often damaging it.

Mosquitoes often lay eggs in the trap water of pitcher plants. For some reason their larvae swim free and undamaged in it, even taking their food from the liquid. As adults, they fly out of the pitchers, seeking their own prey. In northern areas where the water in pitcher plants freezes in winter, some mosquito larvae hibernate frozen in the traps.

Flesh flies deposit their maggots inside the pitchers, too. The maggots feast on the debris in the trap water. When they are ready for the pupae stage, they merely bore a hole through the pitcher and drop to the ground.

A certain wasp builds elaborate nests inside the leaves of pitcher plants. Snails and slugs are often able to spend time sampling the sweet nectars at the edge of a pitcher leaf without falling in. Crab spiders build webs inside pitchers, waiting to capture and eat the pitcher plant's prey. Even frogs and snakes will sometimes crawl into a pitcher for protection, or to steal the pitcher's prey. Sometimes they are not able to get out again. Eventually they die and are digested, too.

Growing pitcher plants is a wonderful hobby because there are so many varied species. Matthew

Matthew Hochberg of New York City has been
growing and studying carnivorous plants since
elementary school. He holds a pitcher plant grown
in a bog created in a friend's backyard.

Hochberg, a New York City college student, has grown them and other carnivorous plants since elementary school. He keeps a bog in his basement and backyard. By now he knows so much about carnivorous plants that librarians at the New York Botanical Garden refer people who want to know more about carnivorous plants to Matt. Reading about and cultivating your own plants can make you a carnivorous-plant expert, too.

# WHERE TO OBTAIN CARNIVOROUS PLANTS

Lee's Botanical Gardens
12731 SW 14th Street
Miami, FL 33184

Orgel's Orchids
Rt 2, Box 90
Miami, FL 33187

Peter Paul's Nursery
4665 Chapin
Canandaigua, NY 14424

Southern Carnivores
5600 Hiram Rd.
Powder Springs, GA 30073

# PLACES TO SEE CARNIVOROUS PLANTS

Atlanta Botanical Garden,
Atlanta, Georgia.
(Outstanding collection of
native Georgia carnivorous plants)

California State University,
Fullerton, California

Longwood Gardens,
Kennett Square, Pennsylvania.
(A fine collection of *Nepenthes*)

Missouri Botanical Gardens,
St. Louis, Missouri

New York Botanical Garden,
Bronx, New York

University of North Carolina,
Chapel Hill, North Carolina

# FOR FURTHER INFORMATION

You can learn more about carnivorous plants from the *Carnivorous Plant Newsletter*, published four times a year by:

International Carnivorous Plant Society
The Fullerton Arboretum
California State University
Fullerton, California 92634

The society also maintains a seed bank from which seeds of many species may be purchased at reasonable prices.

Here is a list of books for further reading:

Alexander, Taylor Richard; R. Will Burnett; and Herbert S. Zim. *Botany*. New York: Golden Press (Western Publishing), 1970.

Burnie, David. *Plant*. New York: Alfred Knopf, 1989.

Lerner, Carol. *Pitcher Plants*. Minneapolis: Lerner Publications, 1983.

Overbeck, Cynthia. *Carnivorous Plants*. Minneapolis: Lerner Publications, 1982.

Slack, Adrian. *Insect-Eating Plants and How to Grow Them*. Seattle: University of Washington Press, 1988.

Wexler, Jerome. *Secrets of the Venus's Fly Trap*. New York: Dodd, Mead, 1981.

# INDEX

# ABOUT THE AUTHOR

Nancy J. Nielsen is a former elementary school teacher. She is now a full-time writer specializing in juvenile books and educational materials. She has also written *Animal Migration* for Franklin Watts. Ms. Nielsen makes her home in Minneapolis, Minnesota. In her leisure time, she enjoys reading, gardening, cross-country skiing, and canoeing.

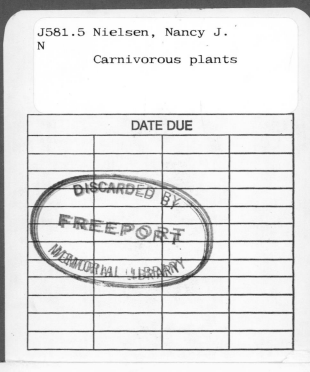